12-14

D0793654

The NFL's Greatest Teams

PITTSBURGH STEELERS

Big Buddy Books
An Imprint of Abdo Publishing
www.abdopublishing.com

Marcia Zappa

www.abdopublishing.com

Published by Abdo Publishing, a division of ABDO, PO Box 398166, Minneapolis, Minnesota 55439.
Copyright © 2015 by Abdo Consulting Group, Inc. International copyrights reserved in all countries. No part
of this book may be reproduced in any form without written permission from the publisher. Big Buddy Books™
is a trademark and logo of Abdo Publishing.

Printed in the United States of America, North Mankato, Minnesota.
042014
092014

Cover Photo: ASSOCIATED PRESS.
Interior Photos: ASSOCIATED PRESS (pp. 5, 7, 9, 11, 13, 14, 15, 17, 18, 19, 20, 21, 27, 28); Getty Images
    (pp. 7, 21, 23, 25); MCT via Getty Images (pp. 17, 29); Sports Illustrated/Getty Images (p. 23).

Coordinating Series Editor: Rochelle Baltzer
Contributing Editors: Bridget O'Brien, Sarah Tieck
Graphic Design: Michelle Labatt

Library of Congress Cataloging-in-Publication Data

Zappa, Marcia, 1985-
  Pittsburgh Steelers / Marcia Zappa.
      pages cm. -- (The NFL's greatest teams)
    ISBN 978-1-62403-365-0
1. Pittsburgh Steelers (Football team)--History--Juvenile literature. I. Title.
  GV956.P57Z37 2015
    796.332'640974886--dc23
                    2013051243

Contents

A Winning Team

The Pittsburgh Steelers are a football team from Pittsburgh, Pennsylvania. They have played in the National Football League (NFL) for more than 80 years.

The Steelers have had good seasons and bad. But time and again, they've proven themselves. Let's see what makes the Steelers one of the NFL's greatest teams.

Gold, black, and white are the team's colors.

4

Ring Collection

The Steelers have won six Super Bowls. That is more than any other team!

League Play

The NFL got its start in 1920. Its teams have changed over the years. Today, there are 32 teams. These teams make up two conferences and eight divisions.

The Steelers play in the North Division of the American Football Conference (AFC). This division also includes the Baltimore Ravens, the Cincinnati Bengals, and the Cleveland Browns.

Team Standings

The AFC and the National Football Conference (NFC) make up the NFL. Each conference has a north, south, east, and west division.

The Ravens are a rival of the Steelers.

Fans get excited to watch their team play!

Kicking Off

Name Game

Pittsburgh is known for making steel. That's where the team's name comes from.

The Steelers joined the NFL in 1933. They were founded by Art Rooney. At first, Rooney named the team the Pirates after the city's baseball team. In 1940, he changed the name to the Steelers.

8

The Rooney family still owns the Steelers today.

Highlight Reel

The Steelers struggled as a new team. They didn't have a winning season until 1942. In 1947, they made the play-offs for the first time.

The Steelers played in their first Super Bowl in 1975. They beat the Minnesota Vikings 16–6. The team won the Super Bowl again in 1976, 1979, and 1980. They were the first team to win more than two Super Bowls!

Win or Go Home

NFL teams play 16 regular season games each year. The teams with the best records are part of the play-off games. Play-off winners move on to the conference championship. Then, conference winners face off in the Super Bowl!

The team's early stars included Ernie Stautner (*right*), Johnny "Blood" McNally, and Bill Dudley.

The 1970s Steelers became known as the "Team of the Decade."

The Steelers struggled again in the 1980s. In 1992, Bill Cowher became the coach. In 1996, the Steelers made it back to the Super Bowl. But, they lost to the Dallas Cowboys 27–17.

In 2006, the team returned to the Super Bowl. They beat the Seattle Seahawks 21–10. Coach Mike Tomlin led the team to their sixth Super Bowl win in 2009. That is more than any other NFL team! They beat the Arizona Cardinals 27–23.

The Steelers returned to the Super Bowl in 2011. But, they lost to the Green Bay Packers 31–25.

Halftime! Stat Break

Fan Fun

NICKNAME: The Black and Gold
STADIUM: Heinz Field
LOCATION: Pittsburgh, Pennsylvania
MASCOT: Steely McBeam

Team Records

RUSHING YARDS
Career: Franco Harris, 11,950 yards (1972–1983)
Single Season: Barry Foster, 1,690 yards (1992)

PASSING YARDS
Career: Ben Roethlisberger, 34,105 yards and gaining (2004–)
Single Season: Ben Roethlisberger, 4,328 yards (2009)

RECEPTIONS
Career: Hines Ward, 1,000 receptions (1998-2011)
Single Season: Hines Ward, 112 receptions (2002)

ALL-TIME LEADING SCORER
Gary Anderson, 1,343 points (1982–1994)

Championships

SUPER BOWL APPEARANCES:
1975, 1976, 1979, 1980, 1996, 2006, 2009, 2011
SUPER BOWL WINS:
1975, 1976, 1979, 1980, 2006, 2009

Famous Coaches

Chuck Noll (1969–1991)
Bill Cowher (1992–2006)

Pro Football Hall of Famers & Their Years with the Steelers

Mel Blount, Cornerback (1970–1983)
Terry Bradshaw, Quarterback (1970–1983)
Jack Butler, Cornerback (1951–1959)
Dermontti Dawson, Center (1988–2000)
Bill Dudley, Halfback (1942, 1945–1946)
Joe Greene, Defensive Tackle (1969–1981)
Jack Ham, Linebacker (1971–1982)
Franco Harris, Running Back (1972–1983)
John Henry Johnson, Fullback (1960–1965)
Walt Kiesling, Guard (1937-1939), Coach (1940–1942, 1954–1956)
Jack Lambert, Linebacker (1974–1984)
Bobby Layne, Quarterback (1958–1962)
Chuck Noll, Coach (1969–1991)
Art Rooney, Founder/Owner (1933–1988)
Dan Rooney, Administrator/Owner (1955–)
John Stallworth, Wide Receiver (1974–1987)
Ernie Stautner, Defensive Tackle (1950–1963)
Lynn Swann, Wide Receiver (1974–1982)
Mike Webster, Center (1974–1988)
Rod Woodson, Cornerback/Safety (1987–1996)

Coaches' Corner

The Steelers hired head coach Chuck Noll in 1969. During his first season, the team won only 1 of their 14 games. But by 1975, they were Super Bowl **champions**!

Noll **drafted** star players. This helped the team do well. Noll led the team to four Super Bowl wins in six years! He **retired** in 1991. He had won 209 games. That makes Noll one of the top NFL coaches.

Noll is the only NFL coach to have four Super Bowl wins.

Mike Tomlin took over the team in 2007.

17

Star Players

Ernie Stautner DEFENSIVE TACKLE (1950–1963)

Ernie Stautner was small for a tackle. Yet, he was known for being **tough**. He played in the NFL's all-star game, the Pro Bowl, nine times. He is the only Steeler to have his number **retired**.

Joe Greene DEFENSIVE TACKLE (1969–1981)

"Mean" Joe Greene was **drafted** by the Steelers in 1969. He led the team's famous "Steel Curtain" defense. They were called that because they were good at stopping other teams. Greene helped the Steelers win four Super Bowls. He was the NFL's Defensive Player of the Year in 1972 and 1974.

Terry Bradshaw QUARTERBACK (1970–1983)

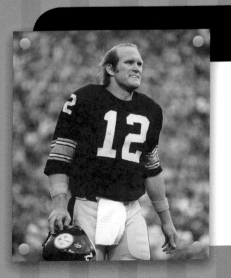

Terry Bradshaw was the first pick in the 1970 draft. He led the Steelers to four Super Bowl wins. He was named the game's Most Valuable Player (MVP) in 1979 and 1980. In 1978, he was named the league's MVP. Bradshaw was known for calling his own plays.

Jack Lambert LINEBACKER (1974–1984)

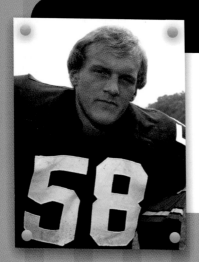

Jack Lambert was part of the team's "Steel Curtain" defense. In 1974, he was named the NFL's Defensive **Rookie** of the Year. Two years later, he was named the league's Defensive Player of the Year. Lambert led the Steelers in tackles 10 of his 11 seasons.

Franco Harris RUNNING BACK (1972–1983)

Franco Harris helped the Steelers win four Super Bowls. In 1975, he was named the game's MVP. Harris is best known for a play called "the Immaculate Reception." In a play-off game, Harris caught the ball just before it hit the ground. He ran it in for the winning touchdown.

Hines Ward WIDE RECEIVER (1998–2011)

Hines Ward played for the Steelers his whole **career**. He helped the team reach three Super Bowls and win two. In 2006, he was named the game's MVP. When Ward **retired**, he had more receptions and receiving touchdowns than any other Steeler.

Ben Roethlisberger QUARTERBACK (2004–)

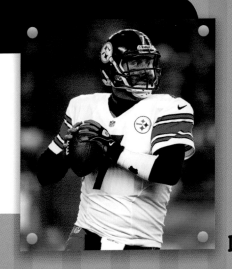

Ben Roethlisberger was the Steelers' first pick in the 2004 **draft**. He led the team to three Super Bowl appearances and two wins. After the 2013 season, he had thrown for more than 34,000 yards. That is more than any other Steeler.

Heinz Field

The Steelers play home games at Heinz Field. It is in Pittsburgh, Pennsylvania. Heinz Field opened in 2001. It can hold about 65,500 people. The stadium has copies of the team's Super Bowl **trophies**.

Some people call Heinz Field the "Mustard Palace" because of its yellow seats.

Heinz Field has two giant ketchup bottles on the scoreboard. When the Steelers get close to the goal line, the bottles tip. It looks like ketchup is pouring out!

Terrible Towels

Fans go to Heinz Field to see the Steelers play home games. Some call their team "the Black and Gold."

In 2007, the team got a **mascot**. Steely McBeam wears a plaid shirt, overalls, work gloves, and a hard hat. He carries a large steel beam. Steely appears at home games to help fans cheer on their team.

Many fans wave gold Terrible Towels to bring the Steelers luck.

And the Winner Is...

The Steelers held a contest to choose their new mascot's name. They received more than 70,000 entries!

Final Call

The Steelers have a long, rich history. In the 1970s, they ruled the NFL. The team became **champions** again in the 2000s.

Even during losing seasons, true fans have stuck with them. Many believe that the Pittsburgh Steelers will remain one of the NFL's greatest teams.

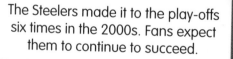

The Steelers made it to the play-offs six times in the 2000s. Fans expect them to continue to succeed.

Through the Years

1936
The Pirates take part in the first NFL **draft**. They choose halfback Bill Shakespeare.

1947
The team makes it to the play-offs for the first time.

1942
The Steelers go 7–4 for their first winning season.

1964
Art Rooney joins the Pro Football Hall of Fame.

1933
Art Rooney founds the Pittsburgh Pirates.

1940
The Pirates change their name to the Steelers.

1975

The team plays in their first Super Bowl.

1979

The Steelers become the first NFL team to win more than two Super Bowls.

2009

The Steelers win their sixth Super Bowl. That is more than any other NFL team.

1974

The Steelers **draft** four players who later become Pro Football Hall of Fame members.

2001

Heinz Field opens. Before this, the team played home games at Three Rivers Stadium.

Postgame Recap

1. What is the name of the stadium where the Steelers play their home games?
    A. Three Rivers Stadium   **B.** Steelers Field   **C.** Heinz Field

2. What important NFL record do the Steelers hold?
    A. Most Super Bowl wins
    B. Only undefeated season
    C. Most overall points scored

3. What was the team's powerful defense in the 1970s called?
    A. The Steel Wall   **B.** Blitzburgh   **C.** The Steel Curtain

4. Name 3 of the 20 Steelers in the Pro Football Hall of Fame.

5. How did Chuck Noll help make the Steelers successful in the 1970s?
    A. By starting daily team practices
    B. By drafting many star players
    C. By inventing a powerful new type of offense

1. C. 2. A. 3. C. 4. See page 15 5. B.

Glossary

career work a person does to earn money for living.

champion the winner of a championship, which is a game, a match, or a race held to find a first-place winner.

draft a system for professional sports teams to choose new players. When a team drafts a player, they choose that player for their team.

mascot something to bring good luck and help cheer on a team.

retire to give up one's job.

rookie a first-year player in a professional sport.

tough (TUHF) able to do hard work.

trophy (TROH-fee) an award for success.

Websites

To learn more about the NFL's Greatest Teams, visit **booklinks.abdopublishing.com**. These links are routinely monitored and updated to provide the most current information available.

31

Index